The Simpsons Of Rye Top, Cumberland Valley, Pennsylvania

Elizabeth Simpson Bladen

In the interest of creating a more extensive selection of rare historical book reprints, we have chosen to reproduce this title even though it may possibly have occasional imperfections such as missing and blurred pages, missing text, poor pictures, markings, dark backgrounds and other reproduction issues beyond our control. Because this work is culturally important, we have made it available as a part of our commitment to protecting, preserving and promoting the world's literature. Thank you for your understanding.

The Simpsons

Of RYE TOP,
Cumberland Valley, Pennsylvania

By
Mrs. ELIZABETH SIMPSON BLADEN
Of Philadelphia

PHILADELPHIA
Press of Allen, Lane & Scott
1905

PREFACE.

I OFFER this story of the Simpson Family to my ancestors as a slight token of gratitude for the heritage of a healthy body and hardy soul which have enabled me to breast the storms and gather the sunshine of seventy years. I have followed their trail from the waters of Chesapeake Bay to the Forks of the Ohio, and their history from the reign of King James to the Presidency of Theodore Roosevelt.

Among those who have kindly facilitated my investigations, I make grateful acknowledgment to Col. Thomas Kennedy, President of Cumberland Valley Railroad; Mr. George W. Boyd, General Passenger Agent Pennsylvania Railroad; Col. Frank N. Barksdale, for information of the old National Road, &c.; Mr. Jordan, Historical Society of Pennsylvania; the Curator of Historical Society, York, Pa.; Councillor George Calvart Lewis, of Pittsburgh; Mrs. T. J. Nill, of Green Castle, Pa.; and Miss Martha Clark, of Lancaster, Pa., for valuable assistance.

ELIZABETH SIMPSON BLADEN.

708 South Tenth Street,
    Philadelphia.

THE SIMPSONS
OF RYE TOP,
CUMBERLAND VALLEY, PENNSYLVANIA.

WHEN Charles the Second was restored to the throne of England, 1662, he proclaimed a general amnesty to the various sectaries and adherents of the late Protector, Oliver Cromwell, but with the astute diplomacy characteristic of the "Merry Monarch," the provisions of this amnesty were delayed for two years. Eminent opponents were beguiled to London only to find that the "amnesty" was merely symbolic; many were indicted for treason and had their heads cut off. Notably among these was the Duke of Argyle, whose son had been received graciously by the King and had persuaded his father to trust to his Majesty's clemency.

This summary vengeance on so shining a mark greatly impressed the old Cromwellian soldiers. One of these, John Simpson, who had done gallant service for Cromwell, turned all his property into gold and came to the New World with a thousand pounds in his saddlebags. He landed at New York, bought him a horse, and rode to Albany, subsequently prospecting through the Genessee country with a view to buying a new estate. From this he was deterred by the severity of the climate and the sight of numbers of refugees who could find no means of earning their bread. So he retraced his steps and finally made his way to Maryland, where he purchased a tract under the charters of Lord Baltimore, in the northwestern portion of the State, which later was, under the survey of English Commission, Mason and Dixon, assigned to the Province of Pennsylvania. The milestones set up by Mason and Dixon in the reign of Queen Anne, marked with a royal crown, are still in good condition in Franklin County, Pennsylvania, on the border of the two States. At the time of the erection of these stones the present county, known as Franklin, was included in Lancaster.

John Simpson is referred to in genealogical and historical works as "Indian trader," though he cultivated a great farm and had many slaves and servants. In point of fact, all early settlers traded with the Indians for the lands they held, as this second payment was security for peace. No doubt they also bought furs and game, but they were in no way less than the lords of the manor, over which they held sway. Of this particular John Simpson it is said that he had been a colonel in Cromwell's army, but he sank his military title for obvious reasons, and carried out through life his Presbyterian conscientiousness. He never allowed a dish to be washed in his house nor a bed to be made on Sunday; feeding the stock was the only work he permitted to be done. Tradition asserts that all his children, grandchildren, and servants were well instructed in the Larger and the Shorter Catechisms, with such excellent results that it is rare to find any one of the name of Simpson in the State of Pennsylvania who is not a Presbyterian.

His orthodoxy even affected the

animals on his estate, as it was the habit of his house dogs to follow him to preaching, when there was any within ten miles, and an aged horse named "Nasby," though no longer ridden, would amble slowly after the family cortege and reach the meeting house in time for the second service. This old Cromwellian soldier lived to a great age and left behind him sons and daughters, some of whom extended their possessions up toward the first gap in the Alleghanies, near Winchester, Va., while the main stem pushed down through the Cumberland Valley, locating on fertile farms, being much given to horse and stock breeding, and

"Gathering gear by every means that's justified by honor,
Not for the purpose of display nor for a gay attendant,
But for the glorious privilege of being independent."

A grandson of the original John Simpson, also John Simpson, is the next to appear in history. At the age of eighteen he accompanied George Washington, in October, 1753, when Washington was sent by Governor Robert Denwiddie to M. De St. Pierre, commander of the French at the Forks of the Ohio, with a letter of remonstrance. On receipt of an answer to that letter preparations for war were recommenced and a fort at the Forks of Ohio begun. This was captured by the French and finished by them. It was named Fort Duquesne, after the then Governor of Canada. Washington at that time was only nineteen years of age and young Simpson eighteen. They were surveyors, and both thoroughly familiar with the route.

History frivoles a good deal over

this seemingly juvenile exploit. One writer says, "The Marquis Duquesne told them to run home to their mothers," but in point of fact the Marquis was in Canada. Washington's commission is on record, and in his own diary he relates how they spent the night with Queen Alliquippa and her brother, "The Half King," at their camp, seven or eight miles above the fort, and that the Indians got royally drunk. John Simpson trod the light fantastic toe with Queen Alliquippa. This camp was always known as Alliquippa, being subsequently the country seat of the late Judge Wilson McCandlass. After his death it was purchased by the Pennsylvania Railroad, being located directly on the banks of the Allegheny River. I have played there as a child with Judge McCandlass' children, Mary and Stephen, but little dreamed at that time that one of my own ancestors had made merry in the same locality two centuries earlier.

Considering the vast area of the great Middle States, one wonders how two boys living so far apart could come so close together, but valleys and mountains considerably limit the distance. Though the traveler passes through four different States to go by way of the Cumberland Valley Railroad from Green Castle to Winchester, the time consumed is but four hours. In the city of Winchester is the Indian spring where Lord Fairfax kept his Indians, and right through the Allegheny Mountains is the gap which opened the trail to the West. In the Shenandoah Valley two of young Simpson's aunts were settled with their husbands, and the probabilities are young Simpson visited them often; hence, probably, the early friendship and association of boyhood and youth with the Father of his Country.

This John Simpson was one of eight brothers. His father, Thomas Simpson, had settled in Paxtang Township, near Harrisburg, with his mother, Sarah, and sister, Rebecca. John was one of the executors of his father's will, probated 21st of March, 1761. He built his homestead in Cumberland County, and was known as the Master of Rye Top. He was also known as General Simpson, whose house General Washington often visited. When the British landed at the Head of Elk, this John Simpson took his sons and his slaves and marched down to aid the Americans, leaving his harvests in the field. These were saved by his women servants and laborers, under the direction of his wife, Margaret Murray, whom he had married in 1761. With him on both of these expeditions were one of his young sons, also John Simpson, who joined the company of Capt. James Murray and fought at the battles of Trenton and Princeton.

While General Washington lay with his starving soldiers at Valley Forge, John Simpson, the father, again took his musket, and with his friends and neighbors marched out to protect the convoy of food sent by patriotic friends in Maryland, and got it safely to the camp.

When he died his household furniture and live stock required two weeks for the vendue. Among his children surviving were Dr. John Simpson, who developed Shippensburg (see Archives), Robert Simpson, who established the first glass industry in the city of Pittsburgh, Mary Simpson, who married Mr. Holmes, Hannah, wife of Mr. Cassatt, Lydia, who married also a Mr. Cassatt, and Isabella, the wife of Mr. McDonald, all men of old families and great prominence in the State of Pennsylvania. The grandfather of Mr. Cassatt was a French Huguenot. He was elected a member of the First Colonial Assembly, a gentleman of wide learning and culture.

This John Simpson, popularly known as General, is still often referred to in the local journals of the Cumberland Valley in connection with sturdy opposition to Indian encroachment; always ready to take the field as a volunteer when an armed force was sent to rescue captives or protect the frontier. He was the brother of

Michael Simpson, who marched with Arnold to Quebec. This Michael was a man for posterity. He endowed a churchyard near Harrisburg known as the "Paxtang Churchyard," and there a great many of his kindred lie buried. He started the ferry known as Simpson's, below Harrisburg, securing from the State riparian rights; belonged to various societies; married twice, had many children, and left an estate worth only $2000 when he died. This probably did not include the realty, and the records of various county court houses show numerous tracts at one time owned by him. His descendants moved to Huntingdon, Bellefonte, and more northern counties.

The distribution of estates in early days in the Cumberland Valley was peculiar; often the children got their portion when they married and set out for themselves. Thus it was customary for the father to build for his eldest son a house and barn exactly like his own, with its due complement of land, and it came to pass that the youngest son frequently inherited the homestead. Many of these old homesteads, or, as they are called, "mansion houses," still remain, the stability of their construction having defied the storms of more than two hundred years. A marked characteristic is the plain solidity of the external stone walls in contrast to the interior decorations. Often the mantel pieces, door frames, and window frames are beautifully and elaborately carved. These houses are rather longer than broad; upper windows are more numerous than those in the lower stories, and a detriment to architectural effect is the unimposing porches which have been added to the original edifice. These are doubtless innovations of more modern days.

To return to John Simpson, Master of Rye Top, whose descendants carry on the straight line from the Cromwellian soldier though the collateral branches are numerous and widespread. His son Robert settled in Pittsburgh, where he built the first glass works and died a bachelor. His son John studied medicine and began practice in Maryland, where he married Elizabeth Edward Durban William Andrews, who was only fifteen years old and a great heiress, having inherited two plantations and a thousand slaves. The young couple immediately set free all their slaves, but as they resided in Baltimore, so many of the slaves followed them that they found it necessary to buy a farm to maintain their dependents. Dr. John Simpson purchased a valuable wheat land tract, still known as "The Head of the Spring," in the town of Shippensburg, where he also bought a city lot and built him a residence. Dr. John Simpson lived in Shippensburg until his death, having done much to develop its prosperity. He also put money in his saddlebags and traveled to the State of Kentucky, where he bought ten thousand acres of land in Greene County, which remained in the family until two years before the Civil War, when it was sold for $10,000. A few years later it would have been worth a hundred thousand. The Head of the Spring remained in the ownership of Dr. John Simpson until his death, and was held by his eldest son, Dr. William Andrews Simpson, until the writer of this article was eighteen years of age, when it was sold for $10,000. It is noticeable amid the vagaries of real estate that this beautiful farm has since then been sold for a much smaller amount.

Dr. John Simpson left four sons and four daughters. The sons were William, Edward, David, and Robert. Dr. William Simpson married Mary Theresa de Beelen, and left one child, Elizabeth Simpson, who married Benjamin Rush, of Philadelphia, of whose two daughters only one survives, Mrs. William Camac.

Edward Simpson settled in Pittsburgh, where he became an eminent member of the bar and a law partner of Edwin M. Stanton, President Lincoln's able Secretary of War.

David settled in New Orleans, where he also died a bachelor.

Dr. Robert Simpson was a physician of great repute, but never married. Mary Holmes, Dr. Simpson's second daughter, at the age of seventeen married Cornelius Darragh, one of the most remarkable members of the Pittsburgh bar. He was just twenty-one when he was elected to the State Legislature, and before he was twenty-three, two years later, to the State Senate, which he left to go to Congress for two terms; was then United States District Attorney, and subsequently Attorney-General of the State of Pennsylvania. At that time the Attorney-General had the appointment of his whole three hundred deputies. His children married: Margaret, Dr. Julian Rogers, of Pittsburgh, and Elizabeth, Washington L. Bladen, of Philadelphia.

Isabella Simpson married Gen.

William Hoffman, of the United States Army. They left one daughter, who is the wife of Major-General Kobbee, of the United States Army. The third daughter, Louisa, survived the whole family. In addition to her own means, she inherited the estates of her brothers, and lived with a degree of style and elegance at that time unusual in the city of Pittsburgh, driving out daily with colored coachman and footman in livery, and her dog seated by her side. Often she drove herself, and every day she took a gallop on her horse "Rocket," attended by her groom. She was a splendid horsewoman, had traveled widely, and was a most agreeable conversationalist. In herself she concentrated all the traditions of the Simpson Cromwellian soldier. Her dog "Cora" accompanied her to the

First Presbyterian Church every Sunday and sat in her pew beside her. She had five dogs, to each of whom she left a weekly income. She also pensioned her colored servants and bequeathed $5000 to her cook, Hettie Jackson, descendant of a slave of the same name, and provided for her sisters' children and grandchildren. She endowed four lots in the Allegheny Cemetery for the interment of the deceased members of her family. Never was there a woman so strong in her principles, love of family, and her native State. A characteristic anecdote told of her relates how, when a fashionable woman was expatiating on the marriage of a pretty girl, Miss Louisa said:—

"How ridiculous to make such an ado about a girl whose father was only an old Irishman!"

The lady replying: "Well, most of us are descended from some old Irishman or Dutchman."

"Not all, thank God!" retorted Miss Simpson. "If you want to see one, look at me, the sixth generation of native-born Pennsylvanian. There is a man still living who was at the vendue of my grandfather, John Simpson, which it took two weeks to dispose of his stables and household possessions."

In early life she was engaged to an officer in the United States Army, but discarded him when, on the approach of the Civil War, he took sides with the South. Her brother, Dr. Robert Simpson, having at his own expense raised and equipped a company, Miss Louisa devoted herself in providing for the comfort of the enlisted men; and when this company was cut to pieces at Pittsburgh Landing, she took upon herself the work of sympathy and solace to their families.

Yet the writer of this article remembers when a child how this woman of heroic mold used to wander in the woods and play with her, taking acorns for tea cups, and crimson maple leaves for dishes, embroidering with delicious fancy those magic hours. In her will she forbade any of her household furniture or personal possessions being sold, leaving them to be divided between three nieces. The share of one niece of personal clothing amounted to twelve trunks full of apparel.

Hannah Cassatt, the youngest daughter, married Colonel Card, of the United States Army.

Of the daughters of Gen. John Simpson, of Rye Top, the eldest married Mr. Holmes, of Baltimore. They left one son, Robert Holmes, who moved to St. Louis, married there, but died without issue.

Hannah married David Cassatt, of York, Pa. One of their daughters married Mr. Coleman. She left four daughters and two sons. The second daughter married Mr. Samuel Small, the millionaire of York. They left no children.

Lydia, the beauty of the family, married also a Mr. Cassatt. They had two children, Robert Cassatt, who married Miss Johnston, and Mary, who married Dr. Gardiner, who was not only a physician, but also a wealthy owner of mines and mills.

Isabella, Gen. John Simpson's youngest daughter, married Mr. McDonald, a successful lawyer of early days in Pittsburgh. She had no children, but her stepdaughter Martha married a Mr. Smith, and their son married a Miss Gardner, a niece of Isabella S. McDonald.

The object of this paper is to trace distinctly the direct descendants of John Simpson, known as the General, and through him back to the Cromwellian soldier, for which reason it has been necessary to throw out all the collateral branches. Many of these are distinguished and wealthy men and women, but their great number of ramifications make the names too confusing for classification. There are the Culbertsons, who went as missionaries to China, where the daughters married great merchants in Canton.

Of the great-grandchildren of Gen. John Simpson there are only five surviving. These are Alexander J.

Cassatt, President of the Pennsylvania Railroad, Mary Cassatt, the celebrated artist, J. Gardner Cassatt, Isabella S. Hoffman, wife of Major-General Kobbee, and Elizabeth Simpson Bladen. The children of these are the great-great grandchildren of General Simpson, of Rye Top.

There are now living of the great-great-grandchildren of Gen. John Simpson, in the direct line from the Cromwellian soldier, Mrs. Mary D. Ritchie, widow of George Ritchie and sole surviving child of Elizabeth Simpson Bladen, wife of Washington L. Bladen, Mrs. George Calvert Lewis, William Rush Rogers, children of Mrs. Julian Rogers, who was a daughter of Mary Simpson and Cornelius Darragh, the children of Mrs. Isabella Kobbee, daughter of Isabella Simpson, wife of Gen. William Hoffman—names and number of these unknown—Mrs. William Camac, daughter of Elizabeth Simpson and Benjamin Rush.

The children of Alexander J. Cassatt, two sons and two daughters, three children of J. Gardner Cassatt, a son and two daughters, children of Mrs. Smith, daughter of Mrs. Mary Gardiner, daughters of Lydia Simpson, daughter of Gen. John Simpson, of Rye Top.

Robert Cassatt, Esq., married Miss Catharine Johnston, an heiress, and one of the most accomplished women of her time. The Cassatts were prominent men in Pennsylvania before the American Revolution. Their names will be found in the records of the Assemblies.

Mrs. Margaret C. Rogers and Mrs. Elizabeth S. Bladen are daughters of the late Cornelius Darragh and Mary H. Simpson. Cornelius Darragh was one of the most prominent men in Western Pennsylvania. He served in the Assembly and in the Senate, was United States District Attorney and Attorney-General of Pennsylvania. His great-grandfather was one of the early settlers, and his father served in the American Revolution. John Darragh, Cornelius' father, was one of the first Burgesses of the city of Pittsburgh, 1815. Cornelius Darragh's mother was Peggy Calhoun, and with her cousin, Gen. William Robinson, were the first white children born west of the Allegheny River. Gen. W. Robinson was the first President of the Pennsylvania Railroad. Cornelius Darragh secured from the Legislature the franchises of the extension of the Pennsylvania Railroad to Pittsburgh from Harrisburg. He also secured for the Western University a great tract of land from the State, which included the vast oil fields. He graduated from the Western University at the age of seventeen, studied law and was admitted to practice, and elected to the State Assembly at twenty-one. He was a fine classical scholar and a man of infinite wit and humor. The writer of this article, his youngest daughter, had the benefit of his constant companionship from three years of age, and can only exclaim: "Oh, my father, I shall never see your magnificent mind and charming personality again."

The inciter to the writing of this paper on the Simpson family descended from the Cromwellian soldier was my maternal grandmother, Elizabeth William Andrews Edward Durban Simpson. All her silver was marked with four letters, and her two eldest sons were named William Andrews and Edward Durban, tributes to her father and grandfather, who had left her great estates.

Contrary to the usual fashion of wives, she was devoted to her husband's family and children, and narrated to me the outlines of their history. Late in life I verified these relations by visiting the old localities, inspecting court records, and deciphering tombstones. The characteristic of this family is that it can be traced in an unbroken line from the first founder in the State of Pennsylvania and that its main branch held its prominence and prosperity through seven generations.

They were all horsemen, fond of land, and lived with unstinted hospitality. The oldest surviving great-grandchild is Elizabeth S. Bladen.

The most distinguished survivor, Alexander J. Cassatt, a man whose reputation both in Europe and America is only second to those personal qualities which attract the attachment and admiration of those who know him intimately. The brave heart and the open hand are his direct inheritance from the Cromwellian soldier.

Alexander Johnston Cassatt, son of Robert Cassatt, son of Lydia Simpson and D—— Cassatt, who was a daughter of John Simpson, Master of Rye Top, son of John Simpson, son of Thomas Simpson, son of John the Cromwellian soldier who settled in Maryland (later Pennsylvania by running of survey) in 1664.

Alexander Johnston Cassatt is the seventh generation of unbroken descent in the direct line from his Cromwellian ancestor, authenticated by church records, tombstone inscriptions, court house register of wills and real estate transfers, and State papers from Winchester to Harrisburg throughout the counties, and from Philadelphia to Pittsburgh. Mr. Cassatt's children are:—

Edward Buchanan Cassatt, married Miss Emily Phillips;

Katharine Kelso Cassatt Hutchinson (Dr. James P. Hutchinson), died April 11th, 1905;

Robert Kelso Cassatt (married Miss Minnie Fell);

Elsie Foster Cassatt Stewart (Mr. W. P. Stewart, Baltimore), and three grandchildren, daughter of Edward Buchanan Cassatt, son of W. P. Stewart, named A. J. C. Stewart, and son of Robert Kelso Cassatt, also named after his grandfather, Alexander Johnston Cassatt.

Printed by Libri Plureos GmbH in Hamburg, Germany